National Moscow Mule Day Drink Recipes

Drink Takes on National Moscow Mule Day

DEDICATION

Contents

Ox Mule

This streamlined, low-alcohol mule uses amber vermouth instead of vodka, which Ott says "imparts an herbal quality that plays beautifully off of the spicy ginger beer and fresh lime."

Ingredients

2 ounces Sutton Cellars Brown Label Vermouth

½ ounce lime juice

Ginger beer

Lime wedge, for garnish

Directions

In a rocks glass, stir together vermouth and lime juice over ice. Top with ginger beer and garnish with lime wedge.

The Blood Orange Moscow Mule

Ingredients:

1.5 oz. Smirnoff No. 21

2 oz. Blood Orange Juice

4 oz. Ginger Beer

.5 oz. Lime Juice

1 tsp Pomegranate Arils

2 Mint Leaves

Directions:

In a copper mug, add the mint leaves, lime juice and vodka. Add ice, then pour over the blood orange juice and ginger beer. Stir gently and garnish with sliced blood orange, mint leaves, and pomegranate arils.

Honey Crip Harvest Mule

Just because it's technically winter (and nearing spring) doesn't mean you can't pretend it's fall. With apple cider and lemon juice, this recipe puts a bright and fruity twist on the original.

Ingredients:

2 ounces Honey Crisp Apple Cider

2 ounces vodka

1/2 ounce lemon juice

3-4 ounces Reed's Strongest Ginger Beer

Candied ginger

Instructions:

Add cider, vodka, lemon juice and ice to a shaker, and shake until chilled. Strain into an ice-filled copper mule cup and garnish with candied ginger.

Havana Rum Mule

For a tropical spin on the drink, use dark rum. Pro tip: For an even *more* tropical feel, try drinking it with your eyes closed and picturing someplace warm and sunny. (You're welcome.)

Ingredients:

1 part Havana Club Añejo Clásico

2 parts chilled ginger beer

2 lime wedges

2 dashes aromatic bitters

Mint sprigs (for garnish)

Seasonal berries (for garnish)

Instructions:

6

Fill a copper mug with ice and squeeze in lime wedges. Pour in rum and ginger beer. Complete by adding a dash of bitters. Stir gently. Garnish with a mint sprig and a seasonal berry.

Blackberry Mexican Mule

Swap your vodka for tequila in this berry-forward blend — but don't skimp on the citrus.

Ingredients:

5 muddled blackberries

1½ ounces tequila

¼ ounces lemon

¼ ounces lime

3-4 ounces Reed's Strongest Ginger Beer

Blackberries (for garnish)

Mint leaves (for garnish)

Instructions:

Add tequila, ginger beer, lemon juice and lime juice to a shaker. Add ice and shake until chilled. Strain into an ice-filled copper mule cup and garnish with blackberries and mint.

Pineapple Tres Chiles Mule

To make an even spicier version of the already ginger-forward cocktail, amp up the heat with fresh chopped *and* muddled jalapeno pepper.

Ingredients:

1½ ounces Titos vodka

3-4 ounces <u>Reed's Extra Ginger Beer</u>

1 ounce pineapple juice

½ ounce poblano chile liqueur

½ ounce simple syrup

Fresh chopped jalapeno, sliced and muddled (3 pieces)

Instructions:

Add vodka, pineapple juice, poblano chile liqueur, simple syrup and ice to a shaker, and shake until chilled. Pour into preferred glass and top with ginger beer. Garnish with fresh jalapeno slice.

Classic Moscow Mule

OK, so you don't want to give up on the classic Moscow mule. Here's the perfect (and traditional) recipe you're craving.

Ingredients:

2 ounces Stoli Vodka

½ ounce fresh lime juice

3 ounces Stoli Ginger Beer

Lime wheel (for garnish)

Instructions:

Combine all ingredients in a Moscow mule mug and stir. Garnish rim with a lime wheel.

Illegal Mule

RECIPE:

1.5 oz. Ilegal Mezcal

1 oz. Lime Juice

0.75 oz. Liquid Alchemist Ginger

0.5 oz. Fair Goji Berry Liqueur

Soda water

INSTRUCTIONS:

Add all ingredients into a tin, besides soda water, with ice and shake. Strain into a tall glass with fresh ice. Top with a splash of soda water and garnish with a lime wheel, ginger candy and a dried goji berry.

Stoli Mule

If you are having a party or gathering coming up in the future, use Moscow Mule Day as a way to test out this drink as the one you can feature at your next event. This <u>Stoli Mule</u> is perfect for any gathering and you'll be glad you added it to your rotation.

Ingredients:

Stoli Vodka—2 parts

Fresh Lime Juice—1/2 part

Stoli Ginger Beer—3 parts

Fresh Lime

Instruction: Mix and serve

'Butterfly Effect' Cocktail

RECIPE: **one-gallon cocktail & serves 6 – 8 people

18 oz. Tito's vodka

12 oz. Lime Juice

24 oz. Ginger Beer

12 oz. Butterfly Pea Tea Syrup

Edible flowers

INSTRUCTIONS:

Steep flower petals overnight and add to simple syrup to make butterfly pea tea syrup. Add all ingredients, minus butterfly pea tea syrup, to a one-gallon vessel with ice. Drizzle pea tea syrup over drink and watch it change colors. Garnish with various edible flowers.

Tart And Tangy Mule

If your tastebuds crave tart and tangy flavors, you're going to love this mule recipe that contains lemon juice, rhubarb bitter, raspberries, and fresh ginger known as the Royal Tart Mule.

Ingredients:

3 fresh raspberries

1 small slice of ginger (about the size of a nickel)

2 ounces Earl Grey infused Aviation American Gin '

1 ounce simple syrup

¾ ounce fresh lemon juice

5 drop 18.21 Ginger Lemon tincture

3 dashes Fee Brothers Rhubarb Bitters

2 Dashes Fee Brothers Black Walnut Bitters

Sparkling water

Directions:

Muddle fresh ginger slice and raspberries in a shaking tin.

Fill shaking tin ¾ of the way full with ice and add all remaining ingredients.

Shake vigorously and strain.

Serve in copper mug and top with sparkling water.

Garnish with a slice of lemon and a raspberry.

Tropical Fruit Lover's Mule

Every once in awhile it's nice to indulge in a sweet fruity cocktail.

This recipe, known as the Oaxaca Muletail, is made with pineapple, lime, and tequila, and will have you feeling like you're sitting on a sandy beach in Mexico.

Ingredients:

1 ½ ounces Montelobos Mezcal

¾ ounce fresh lime juice

½ ounce Liber and Co. pineapple gum syrup

2-3 dashes The Bitter Housewife lime coriander bitters

East Imperial Thai dry ginger ale

Directions:

Blend Mezcal, lime juice, and pineapple gum syrup in a copper mug.

Top with ginger ale and bitters.

Garnish with a pineapple leaf fan if desired.

Bold And Spicy Mule

For those that enjoy a bold, spicy, and more savory, you've got to give the Sichuan Mule a try. The spiced pineapple juice, fresh ginger, and crisp ginger beer used in this recipe will leave a lasting impression on your tongue–in a good way, of course!

Ingredients:

2 ounces Absolut vodka

1 ½ ounces spiced pineapple juice

½ ounce lime juice

½ ounce fresh ginger juice

1 ½ ounces ginger beer

Directions:

Combine all ingredients except ginger beer in a shaker.

Add ice and shake well.

Double strain into a chilled copper mug, filled with cold ice.

Slowly top with ginger beer.

Top with hot Sichuan spices if desired.

Pomegranate Moscow Mule

A festive twist on the classic Moscow Mule. Freshly squeezed lime juice, vodka, ginger beer, and pomegranate juice, make this Pomegranate Moscow Mule the perfect holiday cocktail!

INGREDIENTS

ice cubes or crushed ice

2 ounces (60 ml) 100% pomegranate juice

2 ounces (60 ml) vodka

the juice of half lime

4 ounces (120 ml) ginger beer chilled

GARNISH (OPTIONAL):

pomegranate arils

lime wedges or slices

fresh mint

INSTRUCTIONS

Fill your copper mug or glass with ice.

Add the pomegranate juice, vodka, and lime juice.

Fill the glass to the top with ginger beer.

Stir to combine, top with garnishes, and serve!

STK Mule

Ingredients:

1.5 oz. Belvedere Unfiltered Vodka

1 oz. Chartreuse

0.5 oz. Lime Juice

Directions: Shake vodka and chartreuse, top with ginger beer and a lime wheel float.

Margarita Cocktail

This seriously is the BEST margarita recipe, made with just 3 easy ingredients. See details below for how to make a single serving or a big pitcher for a party.

INGREDIENTS

FOR A SINGLE MARGARITA:

1 1/2 ounces silver tequila

1 ounce orange liqueur (Cointreau, Grand Marnier or Triple Sec)

3/4 ounce freshly-squeezed lime juice

optional sweetener: agave nectar or simple syrup, to taste

ice

optional: lime wedge and coarse salt for rimming the glass

FOR A PITCHER OF MARGARITAS (16 SERVINGS):

3 cups silver tequila

2 cups orange liqueur (Cointreau, Grand Marnier or Triple Sec)

1 1/2 cups freshly-squeezed lime juice

optional sweetener: agave nectar or simple syrup, to taste

ice

optional: lime wedges and coarse salt for rimming the glasses

INSTRUCTIONS

If you would like salt-rimmed glasses, begin by running a lime slice (the juicy part) around the top rim of a glass. Fill a shallow bowl with salt, and dip the rim in the salt until it is covered with your desired amount of salt. Set aside.

Add tequila, orange liqueur and lime juice to a cocktail shaker, and shake or stir until combined. Taste, and if you would like the margarita to be sweeter, stir in a half teaspoon of agave or simple syrup at a time until the mix reaches your desired level of sweetness.

Fill glass with ice. Pour in the margarita mixture over the rocks. Serve immediately, garnished with an extra lime wedge if desired.

Manhattan Cocktail

INGREDIENTS

2 ½ ounces bourbon whiskey

1 ounce sweet vermouth

2 dashes Angostura bitters

ice

maraschino cherries (I recommend Luxardo cherries)

INSTRUCTIONS

Add bourbon, sweet vermouth, bitters, and a handful of ice to a large mixing glass. Stir well until the ingredients are combined and chilled.

Strain into a chilled cocktail glass*. Garnish with a few maraschino cherries.

Mimosas Cocktail

INGREDIENTS

1 (750 mL) bottle dry sparkling wine, chilled (I recommend Cava)

1 ½ to 3 cups 100% orange juice, chilled*

optional garnish: orange slices

INSTRUCTIONS

For A Single Serving: Slowly pour the sparkling wine into a champagne flute until it is about 2/3 full. Top with orange juice until the glass is full. (Do not stir.) Serve immediately, garnished with an orange slice if you would like.

For A Pitcher: Slowly pour the sparkling wine into a large pitcher. Top with your desired amount of orange juice (I recommend 1 ½ cups). Do not stir. Refrigerate for up to 10 minutes. Pour into champagne flutes and serve.

Mojito Cocktail

INGREDIENTS

SINGLE SERVING:

10 fresh mint leaves, plus more for garnish

2 ounces (4 tablespoons) white rum

1 ounce (2 tablespoons) fresh lime juice

2–3 teaspoons honey simple syrup (see below), to taste

ice

club soda

PITCHER FOR A CROWD (8 SERVINGS):

80 mint leaves, plus more for garnish

2 cups white rum

1 cup fresh lime juice

1/3 cup honey simple syrup (or more/less to taste)

ice

club soda

INSTRUCTIONS

For A Single Serving: Add the mint leaves, rum, lime juice and honey simple syrup to a cocktail shaker. Muddle the mint (using a cocktail muddler or a wooden spoon) to release its flavors. Add 1 cup of ice. Then cover the cocktail shaker and shake vigorously for 15 seconds, until chilled. Strain into a tall glass filled with ice. Top with club soda, as well as extra mint or lime wedges for garnish, if desired.

For A Pitcher: Add the mint leaves, rum, lime juice and honey simple syrup to a large pitcher. Muddle the mint (using a cocktail muddler or a wooden spoon) to release its flavors. Fill the pitcher most of the way full with ice. Top with club soda. Serve in tall glasses filled with ice, then garnish with extra mint or lime wedges, if desired.

Negroni Cocktail

INGREDIENTS

1 ounce Campari

1 ounce gin

1 ounce sweet or semi-sweet red vermouth

orange peel

INSTRUCTIONS

Combine Campari, gin and vermouth in a cocktail shaker with a few cubes of ice, and stir or shake briefly to combine until the mixture is chilled.

Run the orange peel around the rim of a serving glass filled with ice. Strain the cocktail over the ice, and garnish with the orange peel.

Sangria Cocktail

INGREDIENTS

2 bottles Spanish red wine (Rioja wine is most popular)

1/2 cup brandy

2 oranges, one juiced and one diced

1 green apple, diced

1 lemon, diced

1 cinnamon stick

optional sweetener: simple syrup* or maple syrup

optional bubbles: lemon-lime soda, ginger ale or sparkling water

INSTRUCTIONS

Add the wine, brandy, orange juice, diced orange, diced apple, diced lemon and cinnamon stick to a large pitcher. Stir to combine. Taste and add in a few tablespoons of sweetener, if desired.

Cover and refrigerate for at least 30 minutes or up to 4 hours.

Serve the sangria over ice, topping off each glass with a splash of bubbly soda (or sparkling water) if desired.

Fresh Ginger Moscow Mule

This is a fresh ginger Moscow mule recipe with freshly squeezed orange and lime juice.

INGREDIENTS

2 ounes vodka

3 teaspoons ginger (peeled and grated)

1/2 tablespoon granulated sugar

4 leaves basil

1 1/2 ounce freshly squeezed orange juice

1 1/2 ounce fresh lime juice

1/2 cup soda water (or seltzer)

lime and/or orange wedges for garnish

INSTRUCTIONS

In a mug or cup, add sugar, ginger and basil and gently muddle for a few second until basil becomes fragrant (until you can smell it).

Add vodka and stir well until sugar has completely dissolved.

Add orange juice, lime juice and a few ice cubes (3 or 4 big cubes) and stir.

Add soda water and give it a quick stir.

Serve this Moscow mule recipe garnished with lime and orange wedges.

NOTES

You can also add a little cayenne pepper (just a sprinkle – cayenne pepper is very powerful!)

Ginger Apple Moscow Mule

INGREDIENTS

2 ounces vodka

juice from 1/2 of a lime

1/3 cup apple cider

1 tablespoon apple butter

1-2 teaspoons fresh grated ginger

ginger beer, for topping

pomegranate arils and cinnamon sticks, for serving

US Customary - Metric

INSTRUCTIONS

1. Fill a cocktail glass with ice.

2. Combine the vodka, lime juice, apple cider, apple butter, and ginger in a cocktail shaker. Fill with ice and shake until combined, about 1 minute. Strain into your prepared glass. Top with ginger beer and garnish with apple slices, pomegranate arils, and cinnamon sticks.

Scratch-Made Moscow Mules + Ginger Beer Concentrate

Sure, you could use ginger beer here, but a refreshing moscow mule made with homemade ginger concentrate is a revelation. The addition of ginger liqueur makes it extra special.

Ingredients:

For Ginger Concentrate:

10 ounces fresh young ginger

2 cups filtered water, divided

1/2 to 1 cup granulated sugar, to taste*

1/2 to 1 cup freshly squeezed lime juice, to taste

For Moscow Mules:

2 ounces ginger concentrate, or to taste

2 ounces vodka

1 ounce Domaine de Canton ginger liqueur

lime juice, optional, to taste

club soda

mint sprig, for garnish

Directions:

Wash and scrub ginger to remove all traces of dirt (break off limbs to be sure you get all the stray dirt in the crevices). You do not have to peel the ginger, especially if using young ginger. Cut into 1-inch pieces.

Microwave 1 1/2 cups of water with sugar until warm and stir until sugar is completely dissolved. (You can use anywhere from 1/2 to 1 cup of sugar in the concentrate depending on how sweet you want your ginger concentrate: if you will be using this recipe for moscow mules, which adds sweet ginger liqueur, you may want to use less sugar. But if you will be using it in other recipes, or drinking it straight up with soda, you might find you prefer it a bit sweeter.)

Blend ginger with 1 cup of sugar water until smooth and no large chunks remain.

Strain through a fine mesh sieve, pushing out as much liquid as possible. Return pulp to blender along with remaining sugar water, and blend again until smooth (this 'second pass' will extract even more ginger juice and will make your ginger go even further). Pour into strainer. If necessary, rinse blender with another 1/4 cup or so of filtered water to get out any remaining ginger pulp. Press through sieve to remove as much ginger juice as possible. Discard solids (or save it to use in Asian recipes, broths or stir frys, for extra ginger flavor).

Add lime juice (if you want more of it than is already in the concentrate) to taste and stir to combine.

This ginger concentrate will keep, refrigerated in a bottle or other airtight container, for up to a month. Stir well before using as some settling is normal. You can also freeze the concentrate in ice cube trays and store the cubes for up to 6 months.

For Moscow Mules:

Add ginger concentrate, vodka, and ginger liqueur to a chilled copper mug with ice. Stir to combine. Add lime juice to taste (if desired), and top with a sprig of mint for garnish. Serve cold.

Frosty's Frosted Moscow Mule

INGREDIENTS

2 ounces vodka

juice from 1/2 lime juice

1/4 cup fresh grapefruit juice, plus grapefruit slices for serving

a dash of McCormick Peppermint Extract, to your taste

ginger beer, for topping

pomegranate arils, for serving

fresh mint leaves, for serving

INSTRUCTIONS

1. Fill a cocktail glass with ice. Add the vodka, lime juice, grapefruit juice, and peppermint extract. Stir to combine. Top of with ginger beer. Garnish with pomegranate arils, a grapefruit slice, and fresh mint. DRINK.

Ketel One Vodka Mule

Voted #1 Vodka for a Moscow Mule by Drink International's 50 Best Bars Annual Report, 2016

INGREDIENTS

1.5 oz. Ketel One® Vodka

0.75 oz. Fresh lime juice

Ginger beer

HOW TO MAKE

Build in a copper mug or highball glass over ice.

Top with ginger beer.

Stir. Garnish with a lime wedge.

Smirnoff Moscow Mule

INGREDIENTS

1.5 oz Smirnoff No. 21 Vodka

4 oz Ginger Beer

3 Lime Wedges

HOW TO PREPARE

Combine Smirnoff No. 21 Vodka, ginger beer, and juice of two lime wedges in a copper mule mug.

Stir to combine and garnish with a lime wedge.

Caipiroska

Ingredients

2 ounces vodka

1 ounce simple syrup (or 1 tablespoon granulated white sugar)

1 lime, cut into quarters

Garnish: 4 lime quarters

Steps

Fill a rocks glass with cracked ice to chill, and set aside.

Add the simple syrup (or sugar) and lime quarters into a shaker.

Muddle to extract the juice without forcing the rind from the limes.

Dump the ice from the rocks glass into the shaker, add the vodka, and shake until well-chilled.

Pour the entire drink, including the ice, into the chilled glass, and garnish with 4 lime quarters.

Black Russian Drink

INGREDIENTS

1.5 ounces vodka

3/4 ounce Kahlua, or other coffee flavored liqueur

GEAR WE USED

Rocks Glass

INSTRUCTIONS

Pour the ingredients into a highball glass with ice cubes, and stir.

Serve with a straw.

NOTES

Some bartenders prefer to pour the vodka, then the coffee liqueur, and let it settle without stirring.

Classic Dry Martini

The classic martini cocktail starts with gin and dry vermouth. Stir the cocktail with ice until well chilled—the outside of the glass should get cold, too. You can use a wide range of gins and vermouths here; keep tasting until you find your favorite. Be sure to use a fresh bottle of vermouth and keep any leftovers in your fridge.

INGREDIENTS

Cracked ice

2 1/2 ounces London dry gin, such as Beefeater

1/2 ounce dry vermouth, preferably Noilly Prat

Green olive for garnish

PREPARATION

In mixing glass or cocktail shaker filled with ice, combine gin and vermouth. Stir well, about 30 seconds, then strain into martini glass. Garnish with olive or lemon twist and serve.

White Russian Drink

Ingredients

2 ounces vodka

1 ounce Kahlúa

1 splash heavy cream

Instructions:

Add the vodka and Kahlúa to a rocks glass filled with ice.

Top with the heavy cream and stir.

Made in United States
North Haven, CT
23 May 2022

19455605R00039